ONCE UPON A TIME I WENT TO ...

BIS Publishers
Building Het Sieraad
Postjesweg 1
1057 DT Amsterdam
The Netherlands
T +31 (0)20 515 02 30
bis@bispublishers.com
www.bispublishers.com

From the author of:
Once Upon A Time I Was
Once Upon A Time I Wanted To Be

www.onceuponatimeiwas.com
www.instagram.com/booksonceuponatime

Design: Lennart Veenendaal - www.idvisual.nl

ISBN 978 90 6369 454 8

Hello explorer!

Where are you going and what do you want to experience? Travelling is one of the most exciting and life-changing things you can do. Getting lost in beautiful forests, visiting every museum in a city, getting to know other cultures, or just sipping from a coconut under a palm tree. Whatever your idea of a perfect trip is, it will always enrich your life and give you great memories that will last a lifetime. With fun tips for doing stuff, lots of pages on which you can write your best memories, self-exploring exercises, etc., this book will hopefully help you experience your trip to the fullest.

P.S. This book only talks about the one country you visit, but it can of course also be multiple countries, a city, or many cities within a country. Do you see how complicated even this one sentence got? So please fill in the answers for as many countries or cities as you like!

 Always write too much.

 Use a big black marker to cross out the questions that don't apply to your trip.

 Be specific in answering so you can help yourself remember things more clearly.

 If you haven't made a decision on where to travel yet, start with chapter 3!

ONCE
UPON
A TIME
I WENT
TO ...

WHERE ON EARTH ARE YOU GOING?

You are about to go on your big adventure and surely there are some questions going through your mind about packing lists, sightseeing stuff, and other basics. This whole first chapter will help you to prepare well —even if you are an experienced traveller— so that you only have to enjoy yourself upon arrival! So sit back, relax, and enjoy the ride.

TO+L BASKET TO THE RESCUE

Did you pack

☐ your passport

☐ money

☐ credit card

☐ reservations

☐ hotel information

☐ important phone numbers

☐ phone

☐ headphones

☐ camera

☐ toothbrush and toothpaste (for long traveling)

☐ hand sanitizer

Get to know the language. Learn to say,

☐ Hello

:

☐ How are you?

:

☐ I would like...

:

☐

:

☐ Thank you

:

☐ Can I have the bill please?

:

☐ I don't speak the language

:

☐

:

AND IN CASE YOU HAVE NO IDEA HOW TO EXPLAIN WHAT YOU MEAN, THIS PAGE WILL BE A LIFESAVER!

1 3 4 5

2

6 8 10

7 9

25 50 100

250

500

1000

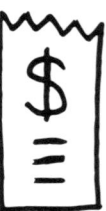

I
REALLY,
REALLY
WANT
TO

see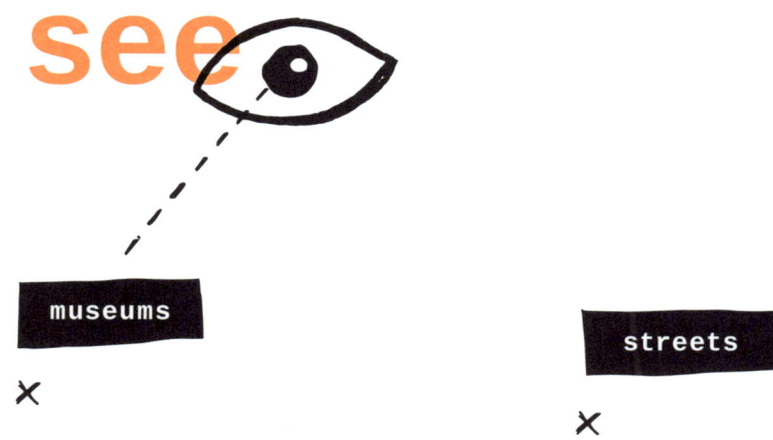

museums

✗

streets

✗

landmarks

✗

sightseeing

✗

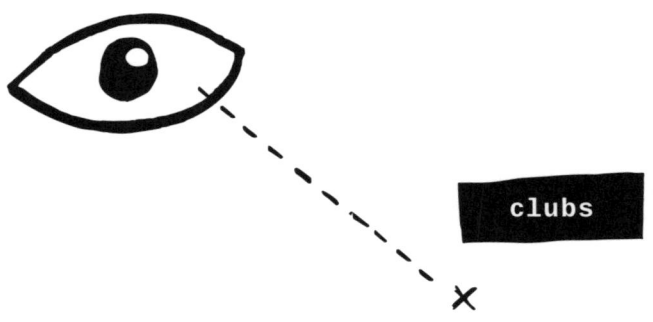

clubs

stores

restaurants

hear

✗

eat

✗

buy

✗

"THE FIRST CONDITION OF UNDERSTANDING A FOREIGN COUNTRY IS TO SMELL IT."

Rudyard Kipling

taste

✗

experience

learn
about

LET'S GET ACQUAIN TED

Think of this chapter as a first date. When you get to know each other a little better you usually start out with basic questions, right? Then you move on to deeper and more serious topics to talk about. The same should apply for the country you visit. When you really get to know the country better, it will also allow you to experience and appreciate it more.

WHERE
ARE YOU GOING

What is the capital?

By which other countries is it surrounded?

How many people live there?

Who is the president/king/leader?

What is the average income?

Are there any rituals that are important to the people who live there?

What is the culture like? And where did it originate?

What is the most common religion? What is its belief?

Can you name five principles that come from age-old traditions and are said to define the nationhood?

1 ✕

2 ✕

3 ✕

4 ✕

5 ✕

What is the country best known for?

What is the climate like?

Which animals live there that you don't find back home?

Which sports are really popular?

Read
a little of the country's
HISTORY

or
ask
locals.

Is there music that is typical for that country?
Which singer or band is really popular?

Is there a typical kind of food?

What is the local traditional costume?

"THE WORLD IS A BOOK AND THOSE WHO DO NOT TRAVEL READ ONLY ONE PAGE."

St. Augustine

WHAT DO YOU THINK?

Buddha said that expectations lead to nothing but disappointment. Keeping this in mind, the questions of this chapter are not designed to get your hopes up about your destination, but it could be fun to compare your own ideas from before and after the trip.

the people will be like?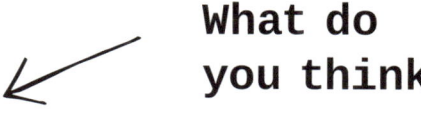

What do you think

...

the food will be like?

the culture will be like?

the atmosphere will be like?

you will like best?

you will not like?

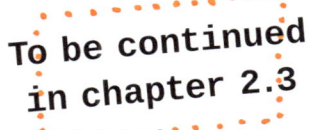

To be continued in chapter 2.3

AND WHAT ABOUT YOU?

It is often said that travelling is a way to naturally work through emotional or spiritual challenges. Don't forget, though, that you are there wherever you go, which means that you have to work on it yourself. But it is true that it can be helpful to be in a different atmosphere and to learn about different wisdoms. This chapter will, therefore, help you to write down everything that is bothering you, so you can really work on it. Don't worry, you will be thankful for this later.

Are there things you want to work through during your trip?

Are there certain aspects of your life that you want to change?

What do you hope this trip will teach you?

What challenges are you facing?

What is difficult to let go of? Why?

Who or what will you miss most while you are away?

"HAPPINESS IS NOT A STATE TO ARRIVE AT, BUT A MANNER OF TRAVELING."

Margaret Lee Runbeck

YOU ARE HERE!

In chapter 1 you learned more about the country you chose to travel to, so now go and experience it! Apart from all the sightseeing you will be doing, keep a diary of your days, try to do all of the exercises, and as you go, decide on your favourites during the trip.

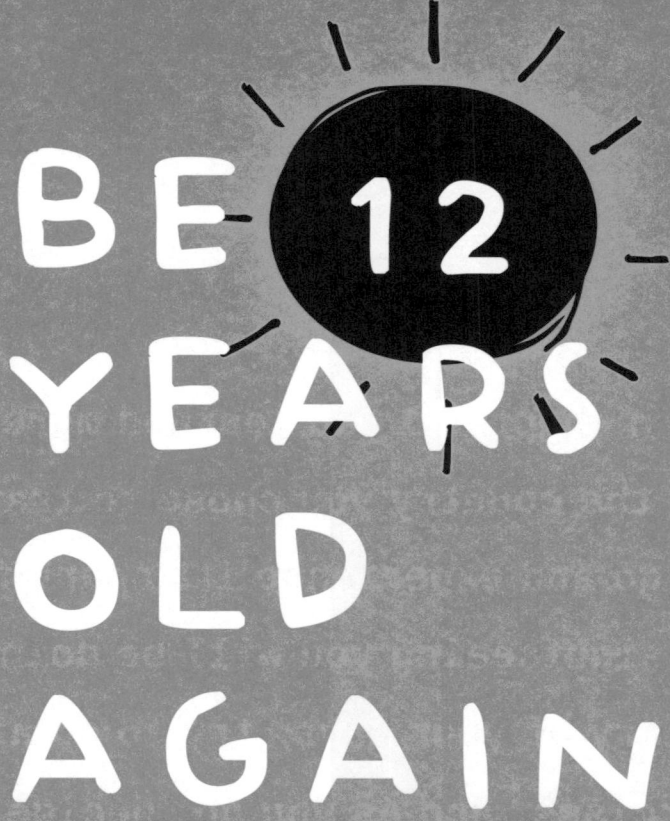

BE 12 YEARS OLD AGAIN

Keeping a diary. It almost sounds childish but it is everything but! Diaries are a great way to write your troubles away, to re-experience certain specific memories on a later moment and to see things on a deeper level. So write it all down, don't hold back.

DAY

· · · · · ·

✕

Where are you?
_____

DAY

. . · . . .

X

Which people did you meet?

DAY . . . · . . .

✕

What were you grateful for?

DAY

· · · · · · ·

✕

What did you eat?

_____

44

DAY . . . .

✕

Thought of the day

DAY

· · · ˙ · · ˄

✕

What did you do today?
_____

✕

 Where are you? _____

DAY

. . · . . . .

✕

Which people did you meet?

DAY . . · · . . .

✕

What were you grateful for?

_____

♡

DAY

. . · · . .

✕

What did you eat?

DAY . . · . · . .

✕

Thought of the day

DAY

. . · · . . .

✕

What did you do today?
_____

DAY . . . · · . .

×

Where are you?

DAY

. . . .

✕

What did you do today?

LIVE IN THE NOW

On a trip we can easily get caught up in all there is to see and to do, that we often forget to actually live in the now and enjoy the moment. These exercises will help you to see, hear, feel, and live in the now.

SPEAK TO AT LEAST 10 LOCALS

ABOUT THE
PLACE WHERE
YOU ARE.

GET A MAP, CLOSE YOUR EYES, PICK A SPOT AND GO THERE!

WHERE DID YOU END UP?

WRITE DOWN QUESTIONS YOU HAVE ABOUT CERTAIN THINGS.

?

NOW DO SOME RESEARCH,
AND COME BACK TO
THIS PAGE TO ANSWER
THE QUESTIONS.

DON'T
BRING YOUR
CAMERA
FOR A DAY.

STAND STILL, CLOSE YOUR EYES, AND LISTEN.

WHAT DO YOU HEAR?

GET AWAY  FROM TOURISTS.

"LET'S WANDER WHERE THE WIFI IS WEAK."

Anonymous

WRITE DOWN RANDOM THOUGHTS.

FOR A
WHOLE
DAY

GO ON
ON FO
AND DO
BRING

x

68

Y
T
N'T
A MAP.

JUST ASK FOR DIRECTIONS.

JUST

For one day
don't plan anything.

GO WHERE THE WIND BLOWS

SEND POST CARDS

TO YOUR FAMILY BACK HOME.

GATHER
5 SOUVENIRS
OF YOUR TRIP.

TAKE AT LEAST 25 SELFIES WITH LOCALS.

X

NOW
DECORATE

ONLY ASK LOCALS WHERE TO EAT.

_____

_____

_____

_____

_____

_____

WHICH BOOKS DID YOU READ OR ARE YOU READING ?

1: _____

WHAT DID IT MEAN TO YOU?:

2: _____

3:

_____

✕

4:

_____

✕

1 **UNPLUG FOR AT LEAST A DAY.**

2 TURN OFF YOUR PHONE AND FORGET ABOUT YOUR DAILY LIFE BACK HOME.

REALLY LIVE IN THE NOW.

CAN YOU MAKE IT FROM 10 AM TO 10 PM WITH ONLY $20

?

COLLECT

TICKETS

RECEIPTS

PASTE

HERE

- - - - - - - - - - - - -

ETC.

GET INTO NATURE.

THROW OFF YOUR SHOES AND WALK ON BARE FEET.

"LOOK DEEP INTO NATURE, AND THEN YOU WILL UNDERSTAND EVERYTHING BETTER."

Albert Einstein

TAKE A PICTURE OF

THE SKY ✕

FOOD ✕

A TREE ✕

STREET ART

✕

✕

A BEAUTIFUL
BUILDING

PEOPLE
KISSING ✕

■ ■ ■

AN UGLY
BUILDING

✕

ANIMALS
YOU SEE

✕

✕

PEOPLE WHO
STAND OUT

PEOPLE
TALKING ON
THE STREET

✕

✕

A
BEAUTIFUL
SUNSET

THE CUTEST
KID YOU SEE

✕

ON THESE COUPLE OF PAGES, YOU CAN DRAW.

Even if you really suck at it, try to draw things you see or you experience.

On these pages you can write down

BEAUTIFUL QUOTES YOU CAME ACROSS, SONG TEXTS YOU LISTENED TO AND/OR WISDOMS YOU LEARNED.

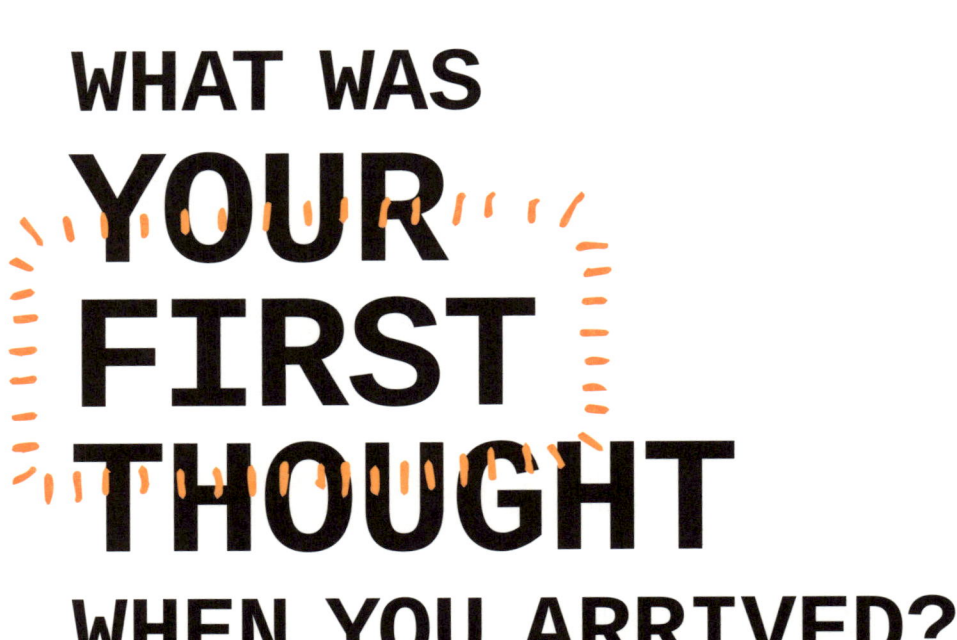

WHAT WAS
YOUR
FIRST
THOUGHT
WHEN YOU ARRIVED?

WHICH WORDS BEST DESCRIBE YOUR TRIP?

1 _____

2 _____

3 _____

4 _____

5 _____

WHAT WOULD YOU WANT TO CHANGE ?

WHY?

HOW?

WHAT WAS I THINKING?

Okay, so now you can compare your expectations from chapter 1.4 to how things really were!

What were the people like?

What was the food like?

What was the culture like?

What was the atmosphere like?

What did you like best?

What didn't you like?

Remember the **five principles** from chapter 1.3?

.
.
.
.

WHICH OF THEM
DID YOU
EXPERIENCE?

.
.
.
.
.

"TRAVELING.
IT LEAVES YOU
SPEECHLESS,
THEN TURNS
YOU INTO A
STORYTELLER."

Ibn Batutta

WHAT ABOUT ME?

Chapter 1.5 challenged you to write down certain things about yourself and your emotional challenges. The following questions will help you to realise if the trip gave you new insights about your troubles (if you had any).

Are there certain insights you have gained
during your trip?

What steps are you going to take to make
certain changes in your life?

What did the trip teach you?

What are your thoughts about the
challenges you were facing?

Did you let go of things? What things?

Did you actually miss the thing or person
you wrote down before?

"TO MY MIND, THE GREATEST REWARD AND LUXURY OF TRAVEL IS TO BE ABLE TO EXPERIENCE EVERYDAY THINGS AS IF FOR THE FIRST TIME, TO BE IN A POSITION IN WHICH ALMOST NOTHING IS SO FAMILIAR IT IS TAKEN FOR GRANTED."

Bill Bryson

WHAT DID YOU DO?

What did you see? Did you like it?

What did you eat? Did you like it?

What did you feel?

What did you experience?

What did you touch?

What did you hear?

What did you smell?

What did you love doing?

What did you feel most grateful for?

What most amazed you?

FAVOU

RITES

Favourite cultural aspect

Favourite street

Favourite square

Favourite sightseeing

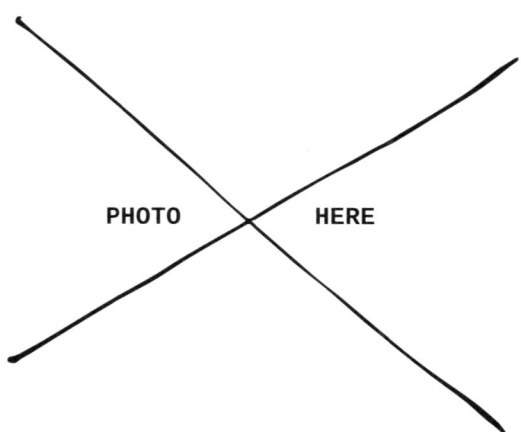

FAVOURITE PERSON
YOU MET

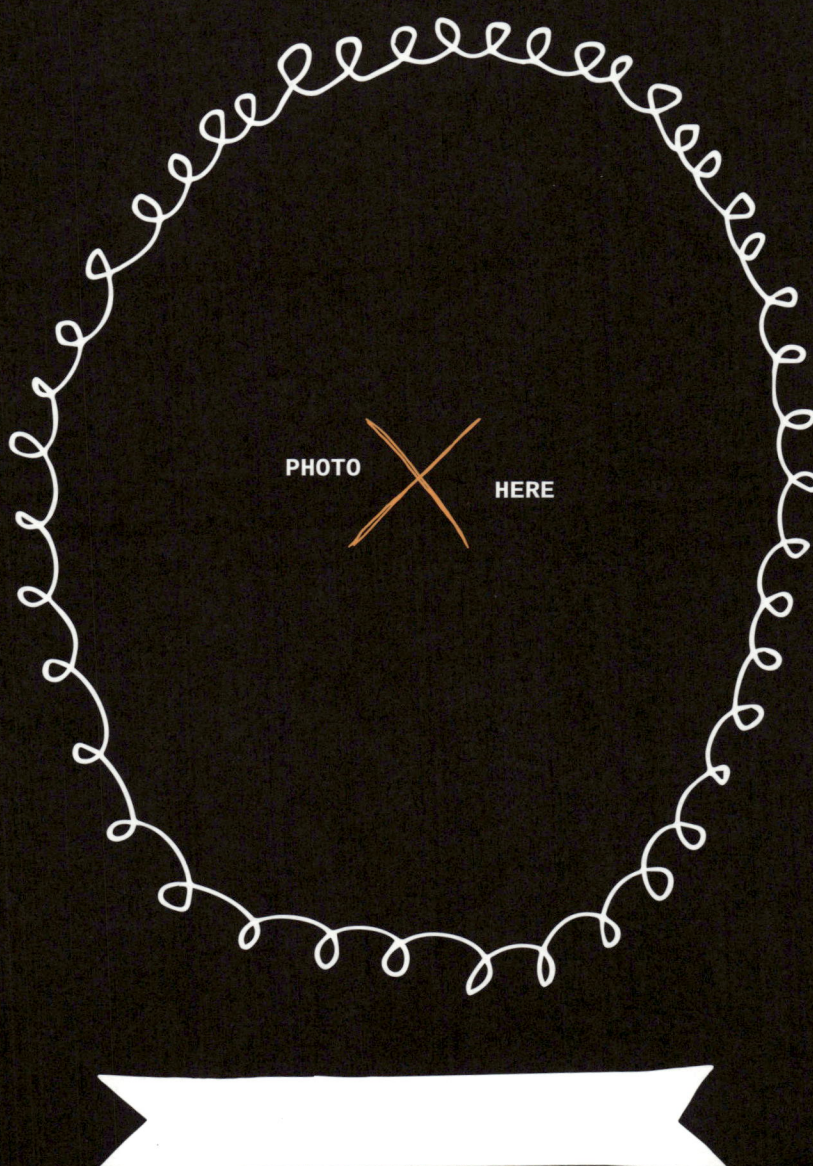

PHOTO X HERE

Favourite restaurant

Favourite dinner

Worst dinner

Favourite coffee place

Favourite breakfast

Favourite hotel

Favourite store

Favourite club

Favourite songs you listened to

Favourite evening

Favourite day

Funniest moment

Saddest moment

Weirdest moment

Happiest moment

This most impressed me:

Favourite memory

"I DISLIKE FEELING AT HOME WHEN I AM ABROAD."

George Bernard Shaw

TRIPPIN' OUT

After this trip you are most likely fired up about taking another one, right? Or maybe you didn't go on a trip yet and you started off with this chapter. When you are ready for some (more) adventure, use this part of the book to get inspired and to get some hand on tips from experienced travellers.

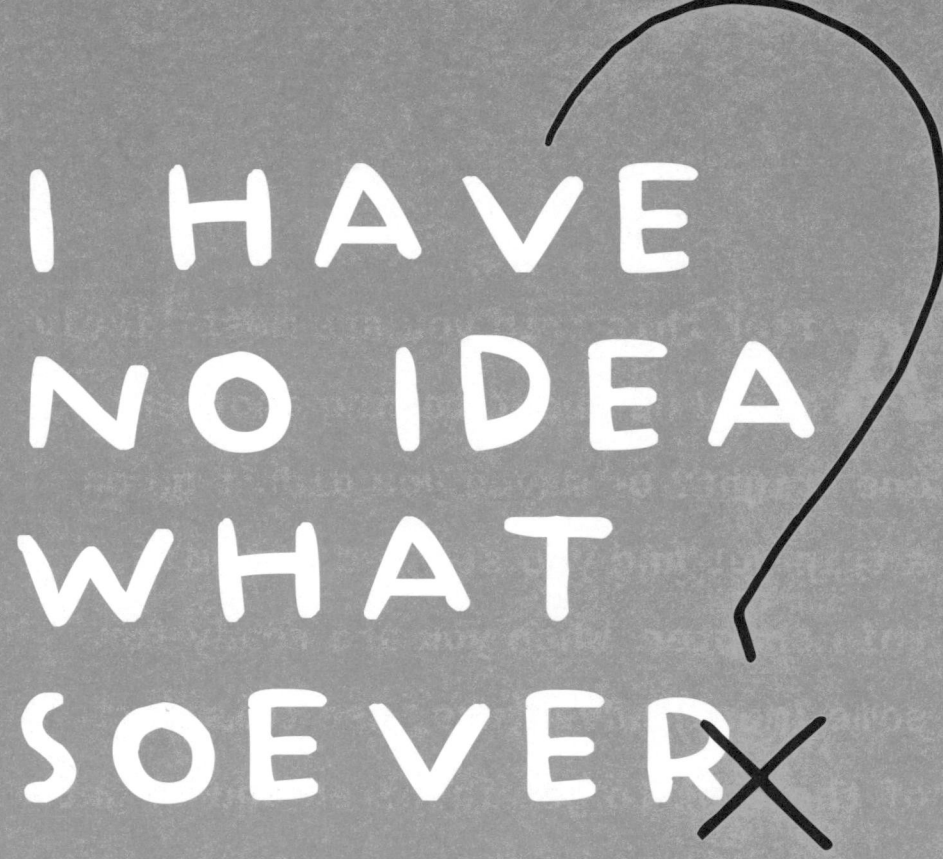

I HAVE NO IDEA WHAT SOEVER

When filling in the following questions, please don't think about money, limitations, or prejudices. It will influence your decision-making process and we don't want that to happen! Also, keep Google close to investigate every trip idea you have.

What did you like most about the last trip you were on?

Which places are your all-time and why?

#1

#2

#3

Why:

Why:

Why:

Which places that your friends recommend interest you?

Are there certain countries that you have always been attracted to?

MAKE UP YOUR **MIND** !

IF YOU ALREADY MADE UP YOUR MIND ON WHERE TO GO, YOU CAN SKIP THIS NEXT PART. (ALTHOUGH IT COULD BE FUN TO CHECK IF THE DESTINATION OF CHOICE MEETS YOUR WISHES.)

IF YOU DIDN'T MAKE UP YOUR MIND, USE THIS NEXT PART TO MAKE A WISH LIST OF THINGS YOU WANT OR NEED ON YOUR TRIP.

SO CIRCLE THE WORDS THAT SPEAK TO YOU AND GOOGLE YOUR BUTT OFF

FOR A DESTINATION THAT MATCHES THESE WANTS.

Duration

A few days

1 week

2-4 weeks

4 weeks or longer

Surroundings

Nature

Countryside

Beach

Mountains

City

Water

Weather

Sun and warmth

Sunny-ish

Not too warm/not too cold

Crispy cold weather

Snow

Atmosphere

Relaxed

Busy

Quiet

Entertaining

To do

Shopping

Sunbathing

Sports

Theme parks

Water activities

Skiing/snowboarding, etc.

Outdoor activities
(think of hiking, camping, etc.)

To experience

Culture

Museums

Excellent food

Nightlife

Theatre/musicals/opera, etc.

Wildlife

Off the grid

YOU CAN THANK ME LATER

To help you on your way we've asked fellow explorers with a lot of experience on their thoughts about travelling and how to experience it to the fullest. These are the tips they gave.

Get out of that comfort zone of yours!

Life begins at the end of your comfort zone. So get off that touristic route, take as little luggage as you can and surrender yourself to adventure, flexibility, spontaneity, and new experiences. This doesn't mean that touristic and safe choices in destinations are bad choices, but you can go off the beaten path whenever and wherever you choose.

* A little side note on this tip is to always put safety first (especially if you travel by yourself). Never do things that make you feel unsafe.

"TWENTY YEARS FROM NOW YOU WILL BE MORE DISAPPOINTED BY THE THINGS YOU DIDN'T DO THAN BY THE ONES YOU DID DO. SO THROW OFF THE BOWLINES. SAIL AWAY FROM THE SAFE HARBOUR. CATCH THE TRADE WINDS IN YOUR SAILS. EXPLORE. DREAM. DISCOVER."

Mark Twain

Be creative

This tip is especially for travellers on a budget and goes very well with tip 1. If you have little money to travel, you have to get creative and think outside of the box. Some destinations are very expensive to fly direct to but when you search for non-direct flights or bus trips you can usually save a bundle. If you aren't so creative yourself, search the web for tips from fellow travellers on a budget.

"Nothing is impossible, the word itself says "I'm possible"!"

- Audrey Hepburn

Explore yourself

Chapter 1.5 and 2.4 already covered this topic but this tip will hopefully give you a little extra help on the topic. When travelling, don't fall back on your homely habits. This will give you an opportunity to explore yourself a little more. Learn about different wisdoms from other cultures, eat different things, get into nature, and really step out of your life if you can. That will make you experience ordinary things as if for the first time and will hopefully give a sense of simplicity and clarity.

Be decisive

There are no bad choices, because every decision you make will give you memories no one can take away from you. So don't doubt too much about where to go, what to see, where to eat (and so on) and just experience it. And if you do make a bad decision, consider this: what doesn't kill you will only make you stronger.

Give back

Giving back can be (and often is) the most fulfilling thing you can do. Be grateful for the opportunity you have to travel and think about the millions of people and animals that live in dreadful circumstances. Search out a charity or local project that is close to your heart and give back.

NOTES TO SELF

• • •

• • •